S0-DOR-426

·TOMMY JENKINS·

Movie TRIVIA QUIZ BOOK

·TRIVIAL TRUTHS·

BARNES
&NOBLE
BOOKS
NEW YORK

Dedicated to my father and mother,
who gave me a love for movies.

The author wishes to thank all those who provided questions, expertise, or encouragement: Stuart Miller, Sharon Bosley, Rick Campbell, Sui Mon Wu, Jeanette Limondjian, Scott Amenn, and Hunter Hauk.

2000 Barnes & Noble Books

ISBN 0-7607-2105-X

Text design by Lundquist Design, New York

Printed and bound in the United States of America

01 02 03 MP 9 8 7 6 5 4 3 2

OPM

Q: Who was the youngest person to win an acting Oscar?

Q: Who was the oldest person to win an acting Oscar?

Q: Who is the only person to win an Academy Award for playing a member of the opposite sex?

Q: Name the first actor or actress to win an Academy Award for a performance that was entirely not in English.

Q: Who has won the most Best Supporting Actor awards?

A: Tatum O'Neal won the Best Supporting Actress award for the 1973 film *Paper Moon* when she was 10.

A: Jessica Tandy won the Best Actress award for *Driving Miss Daisy* (1989) at age 81.

A: Linda Hunt won the Best Supporting Actress Oscar for *The Year of Living Dangerously* (1983). In the movie she plays a man named Billy Kwan.

A: Sophia Loren won Best Actress for her role in the Italian language film *Two Women* (1961).

A: Walter Brennan won three times for the films *Come and Get It* (1936), *Kentucky* (1938), and *The Westerner* (1940).

Q: Victor Fleming, the credited director of *Gone with the Wind,* replaced another director after shooting had started. Whom did he replace?

Q: Victor Fleming won the 1939 Academy Award for Best Director for *Gone with the Wind,* which also won Best Picture. Fleming directed another movie nominated for Best Picture that year. Name it.

Q: What is the name of Ashley Wilkes's plantation in *Gone with the Wind*?

A: George Cukor, who, incidentally, was a five-time Oscar nominee and finally a winner in 1964 for *My Fair Lady*.

A: *The Wizard of Oz.*

A: Ashley, played by Leslie Howard, owns "Twelve Oaks."

Q: In *The Wizard of Oz*, whom does Dorothy meet first on the yellow brick road? What actors portray Dorothy and this other character?

Q: What's the last thing the Wicked Witch of the West says before she melts completely?

Q: Who played the Lion and the Tin Man in *The Wizard of Oz*? What do they want from the Wizard?

Q: How many Academy Awards did *The Wizard of Oz* win? What were they?

Q: Who plays Dorothy in the 1978 film version of *The Wiz*? Who plays the Scarecrow?

A: The Scarecrow. Judy Garland plays Dorothy, and Ray Bolger plays the Scarecrow.

A: "What a world, what a world."

A: Bert Lahr and Jack Haley, whose characters wanted courage and a heart, respectively.

A: Two – Best Song for "Somewhere Over the Rainbow" and Best Score.

A: Diana Ross plays Dorothy, and none other than pop star Michael Jackson plays the Scarecrow.

Q: In the following list of acclaimed directors, pick the ones who have taken home Oscars for Best Director: Orson Welles, Alfred Hitchcock, Howard Hawks, Martin Scorsese, Sam Peckinpah, Quentin Tarantino.

Q: The Academy Award-winning 1996 film *Sling Blade* was made as a short film before becoming a feature. What well-known actress appeared in the short but not in the full-length version?

Q: What family has had three generations of Oscar winners?

Q: Jack Lemmon won a Best Supporting Actor Oscar for the role of Ensign Pulver in the 1955 film *Mister Roberts*. Do you know what his improbable, official shipboard job title was?

A: As of 2000, none of them have won the Oscar for Best
Director.

A: Molly Ringwald was in the short; Natalie Canerday took
over the role in the full-length film.

A: The Hustons. Walter Huston won Best Supporting Actor
honors for *Treasure of the Sierra Madre* (1948). Walter's
son, John, took home Best Director and Best Screenplay
awards for the same movie. John's daughter, Angelica,
won Best Supporting Actress for *Prizzi's Honor* (1985).

A: Laundry and Morale Officer.

Q: What's the name of the movie star character Gene Kelly plays in the 1952 musical *Singin' in the Rain*? How about the name of his glamorous silent screen leading lady?

Q: In *Singin' in the Rain*, what's the name of the studio where the characters played by Gene Kelly and Donald O'Connor work?

Q: *Singin' in the Rain* opens and closes at Lockwood and Lamont movie premieres. Name the silent movie being premiered at the beginning of the film and the duo's sound picture premiered at the end. Also, name the original title of this soundstage classic.

Q: Another *Singin' in the Rain* question: Gene Kelly's character gets his first big break in the movie business by doing what?

A: Kelly plays Don Lockwood; actress Jean Hagen plays Lina Lamont.

A: Monumental Pictures.

A: *The Royal Rascal* is the silent screen hit. *The Dancing Cavalier*, made from the disastrous cadaver of *The Duelling Cavalier*, is the sound sensation.

A: Working as a stuntman.

Q: In a 1988 movie, Sally Field and Tom Hanks were paired as potential lovers. Only a few years later, in 1994, Sally Field played Tom Hanks's mother. Name these two films.

Q: Name the presidents that Forrest Gump meets.

Q: Who was the actor who played Staff Sgt. Raymond Shaw in the 1962 film *The Manchurian Candidate*? Who was the actress who played his "cool as a cucumber" mother?

Q: What was the actual age difference between the actor playing Staff Sgt. Shaw and his screen mother in *The Manchurian Candidate*?

A: *Punchline* (1988) and *Forrest Gump* (1994).

A: John F. Kennedy, Lyndon Johnson, and Richard Nixon.

A: Laurence Harvey. Angela Lansbury played his mother.

A: Angela Lansbury was three years older than Laurence Harvey.

Q: Name the film star and director of such silent classics as *The General* and *The Navigator*, who also appeared in *Sunset Boulevard* (1950).

Q: What legendary Vienna-born film director plays the chauffeur in *Sunset Boulevard*?

Q: What is the name of Norma Desmond's dead boyfriend in *Sunset Boulevard*?

Q: What three Academy Awards did *Sunset Boulevard* win?

Q: Who gave Joseph Francis Keaton the nickname "Buster"?

A: Buster Keaton, who played a card-playing friend of Norma Desmond in *Sunset Boulevard*.

A: Erich Von Stroheim, who directed such films as *Greed* (1924) and *The Merry Widow* (1925). Ironically, Stroheim couldn't drive.

A: Joe Gillis, played by William Holden.

A: Best Screenplay, Best Score, and Best Art Direction.

A: Famous magician Harry Houdini.

Q: Name the two actors who have won back-to-back Oscars for Best Actor.

Q: Who has won back-to-back Oscars for Best Actress?

Q: Now name the actors and actresses who have tied for Best Actor and Best Actress respectively?

Q: What common role has been played by actresses Theda Bara, Alla Nazimova, Norma Talmadge, and Greta Garbo?

A: Spencer Tracy won Best Actor for *Captains Courageous* in 1937 and repeated in 1938 for his role in *Boys Town.* Tom Hanks won Best Actor for *Philadelphia* in 1993 and struck gold again the following year with *Forrest Gump.*

A: Luise Rainer won Best Actress for *The Great Ziegfeld* in 1936 and again for *The Good Earth* the following year. Katharine Hepburn won Best Actress for *Guess Who's Coming to Dinner* in 1967 and repeated in 1968 for her role in *The Lion in Winter.*

A: Wallace Beery (*The Champ*) and Fredric March (*Dr. Jekyll and Mr. Hyde*) tied for Best Actor in 1931. Katharine Hepburn and Barbra Streisand shared the Best Actress honors in 1968. Hepburn won for *The Lion in Winter* and Streisand for *Funny Girl.*

A: Camille. Theda Bara (1917), Alla Nazimova (1921), Norma Talmadge (1927), and Greta Garbo (1937).

Q: Rambo is one of Sylvester Stallone's most well-known characters. What was the first movie featuring Stallone as Rambo?

Q: What actress played Harrison Ford's murdered wife in the 1993 film *The Fugitive*?

Q: What is the name of the politician Cybil Shepherd works for in *Taxi Driver* (1976)?

Q: What is this politician's campaign slogan?

A: *First Blood* (1982).

A: Sela Ward.

A: Charles Palantine, played by Leonard Harris.

A: "We *Are* the People."

Q: What movie has won the most Academy Awards?

Q: For what movie did Humphrey Bogart win his only Best Actor Oscar?

Q: Name the classic epic movie—an Academy Award winner for Best Picture—that has no female speaking roles.

Q: Ingrid Bergman won her second Best Actress Oscar for what film that also marked her return to Hollywood?

Q: Elizabeth Taylor won two Best Actress Academy awards. Name the two movies.

A: Both *Titanic* (1997) and *Ben Hur* (1959) won eleven Oscars.

A: *The African Queen* (1951).

A: *Lawrence of Arabia* (1962).

A: *Anastasia* (1956).

A: *Butterfield 8* (1960) and *Who's Afraid of Virginia Woolf?* (1966).

Q: What is the Keanu Reeves character's "real" name in *The Matrix* (1999), and what is his hacker name? What's this name an anagram for?

Q: What is this character's apartment number? What is the number of the room Trinity is in during her first appearance in the film?

Q: Although *The Matrix* takes place in a fictional city, the street names can all be found in what American city?

Q: Who played the character Liz Teel in the unrelated 1993 television series *The Matrix*?

A: Thomas Anderson and Neo, an anagram for "one"—
meaning he is the one.

A: Neo's apartment is 101; Trinity is in room 303.

A: Chicago, which is the hometown of writers/directors
Larry and Andy Wachowski.

A: Carrie-Anne Moss, who also plays Trinity in the film.

Q: The characters in the 1992 film *Reservoir Dogs* use various colors for their code names. List these code names and the actors who played them.

Q: Name the actors who played the Magnificent Seven in the 1960 movie of the same name.

Q: *The Magnificent Seven* was a remake of what Japanese movie?

Q: What is the full name of Private Ryan in *Saving Private Ryan* (1998)?

A: Steve Buscemi played Mr. Pink, Tim Roth played Mr. Orange, Michael Madsen played Mr. Blonde, Harvey Keitel played Mr. White, Quentin Tarantino played Mr. Brown, and Eddie Bunker played Mr. Blue.

A: Yul Brynner, Charles Bronson, Steve McQueen, James Coburn, Horst Buchholz, Brad Dexter, and Robert Vaughn.

A: *The Seven Samurai* (1954), directed by Akira Kurosawa.

A: James Francis Ryan, played by Matt Damon.

Q: Early in his career this famous actor/director collaborated with one particular producer in the Mercury Theater. The producer went on to win a Best Supporting Actor Oscar late in his career. Name them both.

Q: Martin Scorsese's *Raging Bull* (1980) and *Goodfellas* (1990) were tops with critics, but each lost Best Director and Best Picture Oscars to actors directing their first movies. Name the films and their directors.

Q: What two actors won Oscars for playing the same character in two different films?

Q: What versatile actor played such historical figures as Ben Bradlee, Howard Hughes, and Dashiell Hammett? Name the movies in which he portrays each of these people.

A: Orson Welles was the famous actor/director and John Houseman was the producer. Houseman won Best Supporting Actor for *The Paper Chase* in 1973.

A: In 1980, *Ordinary People* won Best Picture, and Robert Redford took home the Oscar for Best Director. In 1990, *Dances with Wolves* snagged Best Picture, and Kevin Costner was voted Best Director.

A: Marlon Brando won Best Actor for playing aged Don Vito Corleone in *The Godfather* (1972). Robert DeNiro won Best Supporting Actor for his portrayal of the younger Vito Corleone in *The Godfather Part II* (1974).

A: Jason Robards played Ben Bradlee in *All the President's Men* (1976), Howard Hughes in *Melvin and Howard* (1980), and Dashiell Hammett in *Julia* (1977).

Q: Who is the voice of Darth Vader in the 1977 hit *Star Wars*?

Q: What is the name of Han Solo's ship in *Star Wars*?

Q: What famous Shakespeare play is the Bard working on in *Shakespeare in Love*? What's the working title of the play? Name the character and actor who gives Shakespeare the final title.

Q: What playwright is Shakespeare's chief rival in the 1998 Best Picture, *Shakespeare in Love*? Who played him?

A: James Earl Jones.

A: The Millennium Falcon.

A: *Romeo and Juliet,* but the working title is "Romeo and Ethel the Pirate's Daughter." The title change is suggested by one of the actors in the play, Ned, played by Ben Affleck.

A: Christopher Marlowe, played by Rupert Everett.

Q: *Oliver's Story* (1978) is the sequel to what movie? And *The Color of Money* (1986) is a sequel to what movie?

Q: Who played Hannibal Lecter in the 1991 Best Picture, *The Silence of the Lambs*?

Q: Who played Obi Wan Kenobi in the *Star Wars* films?

Q: For what movie did the above actor win an Academy Award for Best Actor?

Q: What was Boris Karloff's real name?

A: *Love Story* (1970). *The Hustler* (1961).

A: Anthony Hopkins.

A: Alec Guinness.

A: *The Bridge on the River Kwai* (1957).

A: William Henry Pratt.

Q: What was the name of the Russian premier in Stanley Kubrick's 1964 film *Dr. Strangelove?*

Q: *Bullitt* (1968) includes one of the most famous car chases in movie history. What kind of car does Steve McQueen drive during this chase?

Q: What kind of car was used as a time machine in the *Back to the Future* movies?

Q: What was the title of the second Peter Sellers Inspector Clouseau movie?

Q: What's the name of the club featured in the 1972 Best Picture nominee *Cabaret?*

A: Premier Dimitri Kissof, who is never seen or heard.

A: A Mustang.

A: A Delorean.

A: *A Shot in the Dark* (1964).

A: The Kit Kat Club.

Q: In the 1942 classic *Casablanca*, Rick tells Ilsa that "we'll always have" what?

Q: In what city does *The Sting* (1973) take place?

Q: Where does the 1961 version of *One Hundred and One Dalmatians* take place?

Q: *The Great Race* (1965) takes place between which two cities?

Q: *The Blair Witch Project* (1999) takes place in the woods outside of what town?

A: Paris.

A: Chicago.

A: London. More specifically, the area around Primrose Hill.

A: New York and Paris.

A: Burkittsville, Maryland.

Q: What was the first movie to use a rock 'n roll theme song?

Q: What song did Hal the computer sing in the 1968 Kubrick film *2001: A Space Odyssey*?

Q: In *A Clockwork Orange*, Malcolm McDowell's character was particularly fond of what composer?

Q: What was the first Andrew Lloyd Webber musical made into a movie?

Q: What was the first British Talkie? When was it released and who directed it?

A: *The Blackboard Jungle*, released in 1955, used Bill Haley and the Comets's "Rock Around the Clock."

A: "Daisy."

A: Beethoven, or as the character called him, "Old Ludwig Van."

A: *Jesus Christ Superstar* (1973).

A: *Blackmail* was planned as a silent, but added a soundtrack for part of the movie at the last minute. It was released in 1929. The director was Alfred Hitchcock.

Q: What is the name of the beleaguered country in the 1933 film *Duck Soup*? Name its president.

Q: Speaking of *Duck Soup*, in what Woody Allen movie does the Marx Brothers's classic play a major role in keeping Woody's character from committing suicide?

Q: In *Hannah and Her Sisters* (1986), Dianne Wiest played one of Hannah's sisters, a struggling actress who also worked as a caterer. Who played her catering partner in the movie?

Q: Name the first movie the Marx Brothers made for M-G-M.

A: Freedonia is led by Rufus T. Firefly.

A: *Hannah and Her Sisters* (1986). In the midst of a suicidal depression, Mickey stumbles into a screening of *Duck Soup* and can't help but laugh—and survive.

A: Carrie Fisher.

A: *A Night at the Opera* (1935).

Q: What was the last movie in which Tracy and Hepburn appeared together? And the first?

Q: What movie featured the first pairing of Bogart and Bacall?

Q: Paul Newman and Joanne Woodward first appeared together in 1958 in what two movies? In what movie did Newman direct Woodward?

Q: For what movie did Paul Newman finally receive a Best Actor Oscar?

A: *Guess Who's Coming To Dinner?* (1967). *Woman of the Year* (1942).

A: *To Have and Have Not* (1944). It was Bacall's first film and Bogart's fiftieth.

A: *The Long Hot Summer* and *Rally 'Round the Flag, Boys!* were their first two joint projects. Newman directed Woodward in *Rachel, Rachel* (1968).

A: *The Color of Money* (1986).

Q: Match the character on the left with the movie he appears in:
1. Sam the Lion   a. *The Searchers* (1956)
2. Ratso Rizzo   b. *Do The Right Thing* (1989)
3. Mookie   c. *Goodfellas* (1990)
4. Martin Brody   d. *Midnight Cowboy* (1969)
5. Jimmy Conway   e. *Jaws* (1975)
6. Ethan Edwards   f. *The Last Picture Show* (1971)

Q: Name the actors who played the following characters:
    a. Sam the Lion   d. Martin Brody
    b. Ratso Rizzo   e. Jimmy Conway
    c. Mookie   f. Ethan Edwards

Q: What was Indiana Jones's first name?

Q: What were the names of Mary Pickford's two siblings who had their own careers, of sorts?

A: 1-f, 2-d, 3-b, 4-e, 5-c, 6-a.

A: a. Ben Johnson, b. Dustin Hoffman, c. Spike Lee, d. Roy Scheider, e. Robert De Niro, f. John Wayne.

A: Henry.

A: Jack Pickford and Lottie Pickford, both of whom appeared in silent films.

Q: "Fasten your seat belts, it's going to be a bumpy night," is one of the most famous lines in movie history. In what film was it said? What actress (and character) delivered the line?

Q: When the lion roars at the beginning of an M-G-M movie, he's half-encircled by a Latin phrase. What is it, and what does it mean?

Q: Frank Capra, George Stevens, and William Wyler formed an independent production company that folded after making only one picture. Name the company and the movie.

Q: "Night Bus" was the original title for what Oscar-winning film from the 1930s?

A: Bette Davis (as Margo Channing) in *All About Eve* (1950).

A: "Ars Gratia Artis," which means "Art for Art's Sake."

A: Liberty Pictures dissolved after making *It's a Wonderful Life* (1946).

A: *It Happened One Night* (1934).

Q: This famous movie is about a revolt started by Russian sailors in 1905.

Q: What 1961 film included the last appearances of both Clark Gable and Marilyn Monroe?

Q: At the end of *Annie Hall* (1977), what actress plays the role of Woody Allen's date?

Q: What actress dubbed Andie MacDowell's voice in the 1984 movie *Greystoke: The Legend of Tarzan, Lord of the Apes*?

Q: Who wrote and performed the theme song for both the 1971 and 2000 versions of the film *Shaft*?

A: Serge Eisenstein's *The Battleship Potemkin* (1925).

A: *The Misfits,* which had a screenplay by Monroe's ex-husband Arthur Miller.

A: Sigourney Weaver.

A: Glenn Close.

A: Isaac Hayes.

Q: If Raymond Chandler had had his choice, who would have played Philip Marlowe?

Q: For what movie did Rock Hudson receive his only Academy Award nomination?

Q: We all know Trigger was the name of Roy Rogers's horse, but what was the name of Gene Autry's horse?

Q: Name Ronald Reagan's last movie.

Q: What actor's character kills Ronald Reagan in his last movie?

A: Cary Grant.

A: He was nominated for Best Actor for *Giant* (1956).

A: Champion, who died at the age of 41.

A: *The Killers* (1964), not to be confused with the 1946 Burt Lancaster film of the same name.

A: Lee Marvin.

Q: Who garnered the Oscar for Best Adapted Screenplay for *The Bridge on the River Kwai* (1957), and what's significant about this win?

Q: Name the first mother and daughter to receive Oscar nominations in the same year.

Q: What famous film director had a role in *Close Encounters of the Third Kind* (1977)?

Q: Who was Keyser Soze?

A: Pierre Boulle had written the original novel *The Bridge on the River Kwai* in French, and was given credit for the screenplay, even though he did not work on the screenplay at all. In fact, Boulle could not write in English. Years later, the credit was changed to the real authors of the script—blacklisted writers Michael Wilson and Carl Foreman.

A: In 1991, Laura Dern was nominated for Best Actress for *Rambling Rose.* Her mother, Diane Ladd, was nominated for Best Supporting Actress for the same picture.

A: François Truffaut.

A: Kevin Spacey's character, "Verbal" Kint, was the mysterious crime lord, "Keyser Soze," in the 1995 film *The Usual Suspects.*

Q: In the 1941 film *Citizen Kane*, who actually hears Charles Foster Kane utter his famous last word, "Rosebud"?

Q: What, in fact, was Rosebud?

Q: What is the name of Charles Foster Kane's first newspaper?

Q: This actor appeared briefly as a reporter at the end of *Citizen Kane*. Smoking a pipe, he has only a couple of lines, but he went on to major stardom just a few years later. Name him.

Q: How old was Orson Welles when he co-wrote, directed, and starred in *Citizen Kane*?

A. Nobody. Kane utters the word when he's alone in his bedroom. The nurse enters his room after he drops the glass snow paperweight.

A: It was the name of Charles Foster Kane's childhood sled.

A: *The New York Daily Inquirer.*

A: Alan Ladd.

A: 25.

Q: Who was the first woman ever nominated for an Academy Award for Best Director? What was the name of the movie?

Q: Name the first African American to win an Academy Award.

Q: How many years passed before another African American won an acting Oscar? Name the actor or actress and the movie.

Q: Besides the actor and/or actress of the previous questions, name the other African Americans to win Oscars for Best Actor or Actress.

Q: Five African-American actors have won Oscars for supporting roles. Can you name them and the movies for which they won?

A: Lina Wertmüller. The movie was *Seven Beauties,* released in 1976.

A: Hattie McDaniel won Best Supporting Actress for *Gone with the Wind* (1939).

A: Twenty-four years. Sidney Poitier won Best Actor for *Lilies of the Field* (1963).

A: Through 2000, no other African American has won Best Actor or Actress.

A: Hattie McDaniel for *Gone with the Wind* (1939), Louis Gossett Jr. for *An Officer and a Gentleman* (1982), Denzel Washington for *Glory* (1989), Whoopi Goldberg for *Ghost* (1990), and Cuba Gooding Jr. for *Jerry Maguire* (1996).

Q: In *Reservoir Dogs* (1992), we learn that Harvey Keitel's character once had a woman as his partner in crime. What is the woman's name, and in what later Quentin Tarantino-scripted movie does a female character with the same name appear?

Q: How many fights did Rocky lose in the five *Rocky* movies?

Q: In the 1980 film *Raging Bull*, whom does Jake Lamotta beat for the middleweight championship?

Q: What actor was originally supposed to play Indiana Jones, but had to drop out because he was starting a television series?

A: Alabama is the woman's name. Patricia Arquette played Alabama in *True Romance* (1993).

A: Two. He lost to Apollo Creed (Carl Weathers) in the first *Rocky* (1976). He lost to Clubber Lang (Mr. T) in *Rocky III* (1982).

A: Marcel Cerdan. (Lamotta did this in real life too.)

A: Tom Selleck. The show was *Magnum, P.I.*

Q: What 1990 blockbuster was originally to be titled *$3,000*?

Q: In the 1994 movie *The Mask*, what is Jim Carrey's character's job?

Q: For what movie was Leonardo DiCaprio nominated for an Academy Award?

Q: What did Forrest Gump say that inspired a popular bumper sticker (in the 1994 movie)?

Q: What actor did Dudley Moore replace in the 1979 movie *10*?

A. *Pretty Woman.*

A: He's a banker.

A: He was nominated as Best Supporting Actor for *What's Eating Gilbert Grape* (1993).

A: "Shit Happens."

A: George Segal.

Q: What's the full name of the character Macaulay Culkin plays in the first two *Home Alone* movies?

Q: What business sponsors the Bears Little League team in *The Bad News Bears* (1976)?

Q: Who provided the voice for Mufasa in Disney's 1994 film *The Lion King*?

Q: What actor starred in both *Funny Girl* (1968) and *Lawrence of Arabia* (1962)?

Q: What president does Anthony Hopkins play in *Amistad* (1997)?

A: Kevin McCallister.

A: Chico's Bail Bonds.

A: James Earl Jones.

A: Omar Sharif.

A: Our sixth president, John Quincy Adams.

Q: John Ford used a particular hymn in several of his movies. Sam Peckinpah paid ironic homage to Ford by using the same hymn in his 1969 film *The Wild Bunch*. Name the hymn.

Q: There have been several movies made about Wyatt Earp, but the one almost unanimously regarded as the best is what 1946 classic?

Q: Henry Fonda played Wyatt Earp in the above movie. Who backed Fonda's play as Doc Holliday?

Q: People always remember the name of Jimmy Stewart's six-foot-three rabbit friend, but what's the name of Stewart's character in the 1950 movie *Harvey*?

A: "Shall We Gather at the River."

A: John Ford's *My Darling Clementine.*

A: Victor Mature.

A: Elwood P. Dowd.

Q: What was James Cagney's first film?

Q: What was the last film in which Cagney appeared?

Q: For what film did Cagney win a Best Actor Oscar?

Q: What is the name of the character Cagney played in *Angels with Dirty Faces* (1938)?

Q: What is the newspaper headline when Cagney's character in *Angels with Dirty Faces* is put to death in the electric chair?

A: His first film was *Sinner's Holiday,* which was released in 1930. He had played the same part in the 1929 Broadway show.

A: *Ragtime,* in which he played Police Chief Rheinlander Waldo, was his last theatrical release in 1981. He was in a 1984 television movie titled *Terrible Joe Moran,* in which he teamed up with Art Carney.

A: He won the Oscar for playing George M. Cohan in *Yankee Doodle Dandy* (1942).

A: William "Rocky" Sullivan.

A: "Rocky Dies Yellow."

Q: Gary Oldman made his directorial debut with what late 1997 film?

Q: In the 1994 film *Muriel's Wedding*, Muriel is a big fan of what music group?

Q: What famous horror actor did Martin Landau portray in *Ed Wood* (1994)?

Q: What Academy Award-winning actor is Angelina Jolie's father?

A: *Nil by Mouth.*

A: ABBA is the favorite group of the character, played by Toni Collette.

A: Bela Lugosi.

A: Jon Voight, who won Best Actor for the 1978 drama *Coming Home.*

Q: In what country were Butch Cassidy and The Sundance Kid finally cornered and killed in the 1969 film?

Q: What famous movie is based on the novel *The Tin Star*?

Q: John Wayne made dozens of Westerns, but he died in only four. Name them.

Q: Name the first Spaghetti Western starring Clint Eastwood. Who was the best-known director of these films?

Q: Name the actors who played the "Bad" and the "Ugly" in the 1966 film *The Good, The Bad and the Ugly*.

A: Bolivia.

A: *High Noon* (1952).

A: *The Alamo* (1960), *The Man Who Shot Liberty Valence* (1962), *The Cowboys* (1972), and *The Shootist* (1976).

A: *A Fistful of Dollars* (1964). Sergio Leone was the director.

A: The "Bad" was played by Lee Van Cleef, the "Ugly" was played by Eli Wallach.

Q: Match the famous catch phrase with the actor who said it:

1. "That'll be the day."	a. Clint Eastwood
2. "Make my day."	b. Humphrey Bogart
3. "I'll be back."	c. John Wayne
4. "Here's looking at you, kid."	d. Arnold Schwarzenegger

Q: What actress rose to fame after changing her original Belgian name, Edda van Heemstra?

Q: One of the most famous scenes in movie history is Gene Kelly's dancing through the rain while singing the title song of *Singin' in the Rain*. Name the types of stores Kelly passes while performing this number.

A: 1-c, 2-a, 3-d, 4-b.

A: Edda Kathleen van Heemstra Hepburn-Ruston changed her name to Audrey Hepburn.

A: A women's clothing store, a drugstore, a music studio, a millinery shop, a book store, and the Mount Hollywood Art School.

Q: What movies received the most Academy Award nominations without winning a single Oscar? How many nominations did they receive?

Q: Ginger Rogers won her only Oscar for a non-dancing role in what movie?

Q: In *March of the Wooden Soldiers* (1934), on what game does Stan Laurel lose all of his and Oliver Hardy's money?

Q: What was John Wayne's birth name?

Q: Who played Babe Ruth in *Pride of the Yankees* (1942)?

A: *The Turning Point* (1977) and *The Color Purple* (1985). Eleven nominations each.

A: *Kitty Foyle* (1940).

A: Peewees.

A: Marion Michael Morrison.

A: *Pride of the Yankees* starred Gary Cooper as Lou Gehrig. The man who portrayed the incomparable Babe Ruth was none other than Babe Ruth himself.

Q: Name the first actress to play "M" in a James Bond film.

Q: What Bond girl also starred in a movie with Elvis Presley? What movie did Elvis and the Bond girl appear in together?

Q: Who played "Deep Throat" in the 1976 film *All the President's Men*?

Q: Who played the voice of the baby in *Look Who's Talking* (1989)?

A: Judi Dench.

A: Ursula Andress. *Fun in Acapulco* (1963).

A: Hal Holbrook.

A: Bruce Willis.

Q: What was the first movie Alfred Hitchcock made in Hollywood?

Q: Of the following musicals, which won the Academy Award for Best Picture?

Meet Me in St. Louis (1944)   *Oliver!* (1968)

Singin' in the Rain (1952)   *Oklahoma* (1955)

The King and I (1956)   *Funny Girl* (1968)

Q: This talented character actor appeared in several highly acclaimed movies of the 1970s, including *The Godfather* (1972), *Dog Day Afternoon* (1975), and *The Deer Hunter* (1978). He died of cancer in 1978. Name this actor and the characters he played.

Q: Sonny (Al Pacino) thinks he can negotiate an escape for himself and his bank robbing partner in *Dog Day Afternoon*. To what country does this partner say he wants to escape?

A: *Rebecca* (1940).

A: Only *Oliver!*

A: John Cazale. He played Fredo Corleone in *The Godfather*
and *The Godfather: Part II* (1974); Sal, Al Pacino's partner
in crime, in *Dog Day Afternoon*; and Stan in *The Deer
Hunter*.

A: Wyoming. Geography is obviously not one of Sal's
strongest subjects.

Q: What movie do the would-be lovers played by Trevor Howard and Celia Johnson see together in David Lean's classic *Brief Encounter* (1946)?

Q: What is the title of the play that *Casablanca* (1942) is based on?

Q: In what Hitchcock movie did Shirley MacLaine make her screen debut in 1955?

Q: Lazlo Loewenstein is better known as whom?

A: *Flames of Passion.*

A: *Everybody Comes to Rick's.*

A: *The Trouble With Harry.*

A: Peter Lorre.

Q: Name the only film in which Cary Grant and Tony Curtis starred together.

Q: Though they only made one movie together, name the film in which Tony Curtis uses Cary Grant's manner and voice to seduce his co-star. Also, name that co-star.

Q: What was the first Doris Day and Rock Hudson comedy?

Q: The directors Nicholas Ray, Sam Fuller, Dennis Hopper, and Wim Wenders, all appear in what 1977 film?

A: *Operation Petticoat* (1959).

A: *Some Like It Hot* (1959), co-starring Marilyn Monroe.

A: *Pillow Talk* (1959).

A: *The American Friend,* directed by Wenders.

Q: Marlon Brando was nominated for Best Actor in four consecutive years, from 1951 through 1954. Name the movies he was nominated for.

Q: For which one of the above movies did Brando win Best Actor?

Q: In the 1994 film *Quiz Show*, contestant Herbert Stempel (John Turturro) loses his championship by missing what question?

Q: What was Merle Oberon's real name?

Q: What city's waterfront is used as the Brooklyn waterfront in *On the Waterfront*?

A: 1951—*A Streetcar Named Desire*
1952—*Viva Zapata*
1953—*Julius Caesar*
1954—*On the Waterfront*

A: *On the Waterfront.*

A: The name of the winner of the Best Picture Oscar for 1955. Although he knows the right answer, Stempel "guesses" *On the Waterfront* instead of the correct answer, *Marty.*

A: Estelle Merle O'Brien Thompson, who was born in Tasmania. She began her career as Queenie O'Brien.

A: Hoboken, New Jersey.

Q: What Academy Award-winning actor studied medicine at the University of California?

Q: Lucille LeSueur was the real name of what legendary Hollywood actress?

Q: Caryn Johnson is the birth name of what famous comedienne and actress?

Q: Name Grace Kelly's last movie before becoming Princess of Monaco.

Q: What was James Dean's middle name? (Hint: It was taken from a famous English poet.)

A: Gregory Peck, who won Best Actor for the 1962 film *To Kill A Mockingbird*.

A: Joan Crawford.

A: Whoopi Goldberg.

A: *High Society* (1956).

A: Byron.

Q: What was the first Hollywood "talkie" (movie with synchronous spoken sound)? When was it released?

Q: Who was considered the "Father of Talking Pictures," despite the fact that he died a day before the release of the first talkie?

Q: Match the line of dialogue with the movie in which it is spoken:
1. "Say 'hello' to my little friend."
2. "Of all the gin joints in all the world, she had to walk into mine."
3. "May the force be with you."
4. "Open the pod bay doors, Hal."
5. "Match me, Sidney."

a. *Casablanca* (1942)
b. *Star Wars* (1977)
c. *Scarface* (1983)
d. *2001: A Space Odyssey* (1968)
e. *Sweet Smell of Success* (1957)

A: *The Jazz Singer,* starring Al Jolson, released October 6, 1927.

A: Sam Warner, because when Warner Brothers produced *The Jazz Singer,* he worked the hardest on the picture and fought for the added sound.

A: 1-c, 2-a, 3-b, 4-d, 5-e.

Q: The shower scene in the 1960 classic *Psycho* is one of the most famous in film history. Name the character killed in the shower scene and the actress who played her. For bonus points, name the city in which the movie's opening scenes occur.

Q: What inspired the colors of Krzysztof Kieslowski's film trilogy: *Blue* (1993), *White* (1993), and *Red* (1994)?

Q: What director said, "I demand that a film express either the joy of making cinema or the agony of making cinema; I am not at all interested in anything in between; I am not interested in all those films that do not pulse."

Q: In what classic Hitchcock movie do Jimmy Stewart and Kim Novak star?

Q: Martin Sheen changed his name. What was his name at birth?

A: Marion Crane was played by Janet Leigh. The opening
    scenes occur in Phoenix, Arizona.

A: The French flag.

A: François Truffaut, who directed such films as *Two English
    Girls* (1972) and *Day For Night* (1973).

A: *Vertigo* (1958).

A: Ramon Estevez, who took the name Sheen from Bishop
    Sheen.

Q: Tom Cruise, Gary Oldman, and Eddie Murphy have all played vampires. Name the three movies featuring them as the undead.

Q: In the 1980s, he could be seen as the lead singer of one of the most popular rock bands in the world. Most recently, he could be seen manning a submarine in *U-571* (2000). Who is this rocker/actor?

Q: *The Addams Family* (1991), *The Brady Bunch Movie* (1995), and *Wild Wild West* (1999) are all obviously films adapted from TV shows. But what movie inspired the popular TV show *Alice*? Who directed this movie, and who played Alice? Who was the only actor in the movie to reprise his role on the TV series?

Q: Robert Altman's *M*A*S*H** (1970) was turned into a very popular TV series. Just like *Alice*, only one actor reprised his role from the movie in the TV series. Name the actor and the character he played.

A: Cruise played a vampire in the 1994 screen adaptation of Anne Rice's *Interview with the Vampire*, Gary Oldman took on the title role in Francis Ford Coppola's 1992 version of *Dracula*, and Eddie Murphy starred in the offbeat *Vampire in Brooklyn* (1995).

A: Jon Bon Jovi.

A: *Alice Doesn't Live Here Anymore* (1974) was directed by Martin Scorsese and starred Ellen Burstyn. Vic Tayback played the diner owner Mel in both the movie and the TV show.

A: Gary Burghoff played Radar O'Reilly in both.

Q: *New York Stories* (1989) consists of three short films directed by three famous directors. Name these shorts and their directors.

Q: In 1985, the five of them represented common high school stereotypes: a jock, a nerd, a princess, a freak, and, of course, the troublesome rebel. Who were these actors, and in what movie did they all bond in detention, thus defining teen angst for the 1980s?

Q: Who played Che Guevara in the 1969 movie *Che*? Who played Fidel Castro?

Q: Actor Michael Keaton changed his name because his original one was already taken. What was his name before he changed it?

A: "Life Lessons" by Martin Scorsese, "Life Without Zoe" by Francis Ford Coppola, and "Oedipus Wrecks" by Woody Allen.

A: The movie is *The Breakfast Club*. The actors are Emilio Estevez, Anthony Michael Hall, Molly Ringwald, Ally Sheedy, and Judd Nelson.

A: Omar Sharif. Jack Palance.

A: Michael Douglas.

Q: What was the Coen Brothers's first movie?

Q: *Blood Simple* and *Fargo* (1996) have something in common: an actress who is very special to one of the Coen brothers. Who is this actress, and why is she so special to one of the brothers?

Q: For years, he was a popular western hero in B level productions. Toward the end of his career, he made a classic western with director Sam Peckinpah. He was also a shrewd businessman and real estate developer who was very wealthy when he retired. Who is this Virginia-born actor/entrepreneur, and what classic movie did he make with Peckinpah?

Q: This character actor played a philosophical cabby in *Taxi Driver* (1976), a campaign manager in *The Candidate* (1972), and Frankenstein's monster in *Young Frankenstein* (1974). Who is this versatile actor?

A: *Blood Simple* (1984).

A: Frances McDormand is the actress. She is married to Joel Coen.

A: Randolph Scott is the actor. The movie is *Ride the High Country* (1962).

A: Peter Boyle.